The Science of
RENEWABLE
ENERGY

THE SCIENCE OF
WIND
ENERGY

by Maddie Spalding

ReferencePoint
Press®

WITHDRAWN

San Diego, CA

© 2018 ReferencePoint Press, Inc.
Printed in the United States

For more information, contact:
ReferencePoint Press, Inc.
PO Box 27779
San Diego, CA 92198
www.ReferencePointPress.com

Library of Congress Cataloging-in-Publication Data

Names: Spalding, Maddie, 1990- author.
Title: The science of wind energy / by Maddie Spalding.
Description: San Diego, CA : ReferencePoint Press, Inc., [2018] | Series: The
    science of renewable energy | Includes bibliographical references and
    index.
Identifiers: LCCN 2017042008| ISBN 9781682823095 (hardcover : alk. paper) |
    ISBN 9781682823101 (pdf)
Subjects: LCSH: Wind power--Juvenile literature.
Classification: LCC TJ820 .S646 2018 | DDC 621.31/2136--dc23
LC record available at https://lccn.loc.gov/2017042008

IMPORTANT EVENTS IN THE DEVELOPMENT OF
WIND ENERGY

1931
French engineer G. J. M. Darrieus invents the Darrieus vertical-axis turbine.

1991
The world's first offshore wind farm, built off the coast of southern Denmark, begins supplying energy to the local power grid.

1922
Finnish engineer S. J. Savonius invents the Savonius vertical-axis turbine.

1970s
Political conflicts over oil in the Middle East lead to widespread oil shortages. As a result, governments begin investing more in alternative energies, including wind energy.

1880	1920	1940	1960	1970

1887
Scottish engineer James Blyth builds the first electricity-generating windmill.

1941
The world's first large-scale wind turbine, called the Smith-Putnam turbine, is connected to the power grid in Castleton, Vermont.

4

2008
Rock Port, Missouri, becomes the first US town to be powered completely by wind.

2016
Block Island Wind Farm, the first offshore wind farm in the United States, begins generating electricity.

2013
The International Energy Agency predicts that wind power could supply up to 18 percent of the world's electricity needs by 2050.

1980	1990	2000	2010	2020

2009
The world's first large-scale floating wind turbine is installed off the coast of Norway, in the North Sea.

2014
Altaeros Energies develops the world's first commercial airborne wind turbine, called the Buoyant Air Turbine (BAT).

1992
The Production Tax Credit (PTC), part of the Energy Policy Act, is implemented in the United States. This tax credit helps drive down the costs of turbine development.

2013
The first grid-connected, floating offshore wind turbine in the United States is installed off the coast of Maine.

BLOCK ISLAND
WIND FARM

FROM THEORY TO APPLICATION

The Sun heats up Earth and the air that surrounds the planet. Warm air expands and rises. Cool air condenses and sinks. This creates a constant flow of wind in Earth's atmosphere. Moving air has kinetic energy, or the energy of motion. Wind turbines can convert this kinetic energy into electrical power. A wind turbine typically has two or three blades. Wind turns the turbine's blades. The blades are connected to a main shaft in the turbine tower. The shaft spins gears that increase the speed of the rotation. A **generator** then converts this rotational energy into electricity. An electric current travels through cables to the base of the turbine. From there, underground cables transport the current into a power grid. Consumers then use this electricity to power their homes and businesses.

In the early morning hours of May 1, 2017, an island off the coast of Rhode Island went completely dark. Local power company employees had shut down the generators at Block Island's power plant. They prepared to transfer electrical power over to a new grid system. An underwater cable connected Block Island's offshore wind farm to the island and to the state's mainland power grid. Wind would replace fossil fuels as the main source of electricity on the island, and some of the electricity generated would also be supplied to the mainland. The transfer was made swiftly and successfully. Block Island Wind Farm became the first operational offshore wind farm in the United States.

Block Island Wind Farm consists of five turbines that rise 589 feet (180 m) above the surface of the ocean. That is approximately twice the height of the Statue of Liberty and larger than any onshore wind turbine in the United States. The wind farm harnesses energy from the strong winds that sweep across the Atlantic Ocean. In the past, these powerful winds have caused shipwrecks. However, offshore wind developer Deepwater Wind recognized the benefits of capturing this energy and turning it into a **renewable** resource. The developer noted that the wind farm would provide "reliable, renewable energy that will reduce island electric rates by an estimated 40 percent and diversify Rhode Island's power supply."[1]

Though relatively small in size, Block Island Wind Farm was regarded by many as a major development in the US wind industry. Europe pioneered offshore wind power. In 1991, Vindeby Offshore Wind Farm off the coast of Denmark became operational.

The Block Island Wind Farm's turbines feature platforms for workers. This allows crews to access the turbines for maintenance or repairs.

Strong opponents and legal battles kept the United States from following suit. Many landowners worried that offshore wind turbines would obstruct their views and be an eyesore. High costs were also an obstacle to offshore wind farm development in the United States. Finally, in 2015, construction began on Block Island Wind Farm. Partly because of the small number of turbines and their distance from the US mainland, the project was approved. Block Island Wind Farm is approximately 12 miles (19 km) south of the coast of Rhode Island, which is far enough away that most people cannot see the turbines from the mainland.

Before the wind farm was installed, Block Island's power grid was isolated from the mainland. The island's 2,000 residents relied on **diesel fuel** as a source of electricity. Each year, the island's power plant burned approximately 1 million gallons (3.8 million L) of diesel fuel. However, relying on diesel came with both monetary and environmental costs. In July 2016, generators at the power plant caught fire after an oil leak.

WORDS IN CONTEXT

diesel fuel
A type of fossil fuel used by diesel engines.

8

The damage led to power outages during the island's peak tourism season. Block Island Power Company spent more than $100,000 to rent new diesel generators, and electricity costs on the island spiked.

With the development of Block Island Wind Farm, the United States joined 13 other countries that had installed offshore wind farms. Although it is smaller than many offshore wind farms in other countries, Block Island Wind Farm demonstrates a commitment to developing the US offshore wind market. Both corporations and politicians took notice. General Electric executive Jerome Pecresse said, "It is the beginning of a new market. It can prove that offshore wind can be done."[2] Sheldon Whitehouse, a US senator for Rhode Island, recognized the important development, too: "This is a historic milestone for reducing our nation's dependence on fossil fuels, and I couldn't be more thrilled that it's happening here in the Ocean State."[3]

The State of Wind Power Today

Block Island Wind Farm represents one kind of modern development in the ever-growing wind power industry. Wind farms and individual turbines are used globally to generate electricity. They can replace methods of energy production that involve fossil fuels, such as coal and natural gas, partially offsetting the **emissions** that would otherwise be generated. Most large, utility-scale wind turbines produce more than 1 megawatt of electricity. Each turbine in

WORDS IN CONTEXT

emissions
Something, such as gas, that is given off from a source.

9

Block Island Wind Farm has the capacity to generate 6 megawatts of electricity.

Utility-scale wind turbines do not typically operate individually. They are usually grouped into wind farms. Collectively, a wind farm has the capacity to power thousands of homes and businesses. Block Island Wind Farm's five turbines can produce a total of 30 megawatts of electricity, which can power about 17,000 homes.

Other modern wind power developments include distributed turbine systems. These small-scale turbines each produce 1 megawatt or less of electricity. Distributed turbine systems are used within communities to power individual homes, small businesses, farms, or public facilities. Energy companies worldwide are also developing and testing new technologies, such as airborne wind turbines, that may increase efficiency and reduce costs.

Wind power currently supplies approximately 2.5 percent of global electricity demand. According to the International Energy Agency, wind power may generate approximately 18 percent of the world's electricity by 2050. Improvements in turbine technology have made wind energy more affordable. Many large corporations, such as Google, have invested in wind energy. Explaining the decision to focus on renewable energy, Google executive Joe Kava said there was more to the decision than environmentalism: "It's good for the economy, good for business and good for our shareholders."[4]

Although wind is a clean source of energy and has proved to be generally cost-effective, wind power does not come without disadvantages. Wind farms can be noisy, and individuals living nearby may feel that turbines disrupt the scenery of a landscape. Wind turbines are typically installed in rural locations since winds are stronger and more constant in these areas. Getting their electricity to urban areas can be difficult. Transmission lines need to be built and transported to these remote sites. Travel and maintenance can be costly, which increases the cost of the initial investment. In addition, wind power can be **intermittent**, since wind speeds are not constant. Energy and technology companies continue to develop ways to address these disadvantages.

If the wind power industry expands as predicted, wind may become a major energy source in the twenty-first century. Bent Christensen of technology company Siemens Wind Power believes that the future of wind power is promising. "If we just go ten years back," Christensen says, "nobody could imagine what we're doing today."[5]

HOW DOES WIND POWER WORK?

The Sun radiates heat. Wind is formed by the Sun's uneven heating of Earth's surface. This means that in a sense, wind power is a form of solar energy. During the daytime, air above land heats up more quickly than the air above lakes, oceans, and other bodies of water. This is because land and water absorb the Sun's energy at different rates. Heat causes air molecules to move faster, so warm air expands and rises. When air molecules rise in the atmosphere, this creates an area of low pressure. Cool air, on the other hand, is denser than warm air. As warm air rises, cool air sinks down to take its place. Cool air creates areas of high pressure in the atmosphere. During the nighttime, air cools more quickly over land than over water. In this way, winds are reversed at night. This wind pattern is referred to as the wind cycle.

Onshore wind turbines are usually installed in flat rural areas, such as plains. Plains are typically treeless, and rural areas often have few buildings, which allows winds to sweep through relatively

Convection Currents and Global Winds

No matter how fast the average wind speed in an area, wind speed is not constant. It varies depending upon the time of day and the season. As the Sun heats up parts of the atmosphere more than others, cool air sinks and warm air rises. These convection currents are strongest during the day while the Sun is above the horizon. When the Sun sets at night, the air cools, which results in smaller air pressure differences and therefore weaker wind currents.

Wind patterns also vary seasonally. Winds are typically strongest during the winter season. Polar regions receive the least amount of sunlight in winter, whereas regions near the equator receive the same amount of sunlight year-round. This results in greater global temperature differences that affect jet streams. A jet stream is an area of fast-moving winds high up in Earth's atmosphere. The National Weather Service describes jet streams as being like "rivers of air." Turbines are not tall enough to tap directly into jet streams, but jet streams affect all the wind in the region. The polar jet stream moves south toward the equator in winter, and the pressure differences between cool and warm air fronts result in changes in weather patterns. This changing weather creates the winds that turn turbines faster.

"The Jet Stream," *National Weather Service,* n.d. www.weather.gov.

unobstructed. A turbine tower is vertical and is usually made from steel or concrete, which makes the structure sturdy enough to withstand high wind speeds. Winds high above Earth's surface are stronger and more consistent than those at ground level. Wind turbines are tall so that they can harness these strong winds.

The amount of electricity a turbine can generate depends

WORDS IN CONTEXT

convection

The process in which warm air rises and cool air sinks, creating constant movement.

on the length of its blades and the consistency and speed of the surrounding wind. Long blades can sweep a large area, which means that they are struck by more wind than turbines with shorter blades. They can capture more of the wind's kinetic energy. The length of a blade on a wind turbine is typically one-third of the height of its tower. Blades are usually made of lightweight materials such as fiberglass or carbon fiber. They have an airfoil design, which is the same design used for airplane wings or propellers. In an airfoil design, one side of a blade is more curved than the other side. Wind sweeps over both sides of the blade. As air flows around a blade, it creates two types of **aerodynamic forces**: drag force and lift force. Wind that travels over the curved surface of the blade moves faster than wind traveling over the other side of the blade. A pocket of low-pressure air forms above the curved side of the blade. The low-pressure area pulls the blade in the downwind direction. This effect is the lift force. Wind pushes against the other side of the blade, creating an area of high pressure. This force attempts to slow down the blade, and it acts counter to the lift force. It is called drag force. Lift is the stronger force, so it overcomes the drag force. Lift force causes the blade to turn.

WORDS IN CONTEXT

aerodynamic forces
The forces exerted by the pressure of air on an object.

Wind turbine blades are part of a mechanism called a rotor. The rotor consists of the turbine blades and the hub. The hub holds the blades in place. While the blades spin, a wind vane on top of the tower measures the angle and direction of the wind. The wind vane

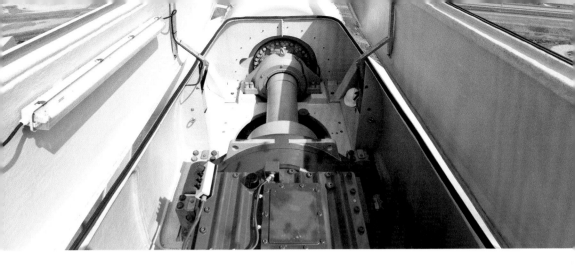

Inside a wind turbine, machinery turns the energy of motion into electricity. The electricity then travels down to the ground and out to consumers.

communicates this information to a yaw drive. The yaw drive contains a gearbox that is powered by the yaw motor. The yaw drive then rotates the top part of the turbine, including the rotor, into the direction of the wind. When a turbine faces directly into the wind, it is able to harness the maximum amount of wind energy available at a given time. This in turn maximizes the turbine's electricity output.

In addition to wind direction, other essential data that helps a wind turbine operate efficiently is wind **velocity**. A small device on top of the wind vane measures wind speed. This device is called an anemometer. An anemometer consists of three cups mounted on horizontal arms. The horizontal arms are attached to a vertical rod. Wind rotates the cups and spins the rod. The faster the wind blows, the faster the rod will spin. The anemometer calculates the number of times the rod rotates over a set period of time. This calculation gives the wind speed. The anemometer transmits this information to another part of the turbine called the controller. The controller is responsible for starting and stopping the operation of the turbine. A device called a pitch system controls the angle of the blades. In low-speed winds, the pitch system turns the blades so that they are at a steep angle. The wind then encounters more of the blades' surface area, which results in maximum wind force on the blades.

The wind speeds required to activate a wind turbine depend upon the turbine's size. The blades on utility-scale turbines typically start spinning at wind speeds of 7 to 9 miles per hour (11 to 14 km/h). Smaller wind turbines can operate at lower wind speeds. Because their blades are shorter and smaller, less wind power is required to turn them. Small-scale turbine blades can start spinning in wind speeds as low as 5 miles per hour (8 km/h).

Blades on all types and models of turbines cannot handle wind speeds of more than 55 miles per hour (89 km/h). If the wind reaches these speeds, the controller shuts down the system to prevent the blades from becoming damaged. In case of other emergencies that would damage the turbine, a brake can stop the rotor.

A wind turbine's rotor is attached to a low-speed shaft. This shaft turns at a rate of about 30 to 60 revolutions per minute. This is not fast enough to generate electricity. The low-speed shaft spins a group of gears inside the turbine called a gearbox. The gearbox connects the low-speed shaft to a high-speed shaft. The low-speed shaft, high-speed shaft, and gearbox are all in a part of the turbine called the nacelle. The nacelle is a cylindrical or box-shaped structure typically made out of fiberglass. It protects the machinery contained within. Inside the nacelle, the gears increase the rotation speed of the high-speed shaft to about 1,000 to 1,800 rotations per minute. At these speeds, most generators can produce electricity. The high-speed shaft drives the generator. A generator consists of copper wires and magnets. The magnets create a magnetic field, and the wires spin inside this magnetic field. This process generates electricity.

The electrical current travels down the interior of the tower as **direct current** (DC). A converter at the base of the turbine converts the direct current to **alternating current** (AC), which is the most commonly used kind of current. A device called a transformer then increases the voltage, or intensity, of the current. The current travels through underground cables to a substation. Transformers within a substation increase the voltage even more, and the strong current is then distributed from the substation into a power grid. A power grid consists of transmission lines that send electricity into homes and businesses.

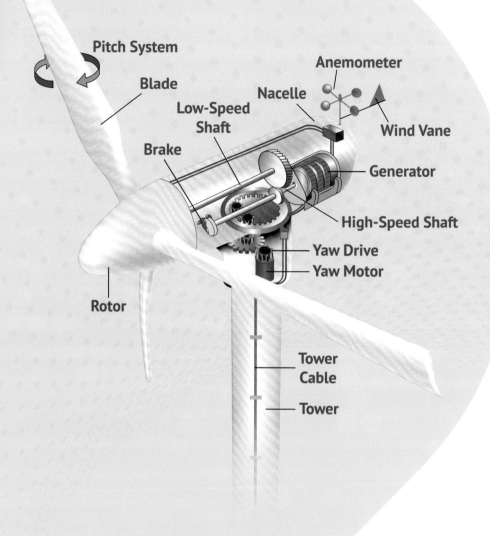

Pitch System

Anemometer

Blade

Nacelle

Low-Speed Shaft

Wind Vane

Brake

Generator

High-Speed Shaft

Yaw Drive

Yaw Motor

Rotor

Tower Cable

Tower

Inside a Wind Turbine

Harnessing the Power of Wind

As the US Department of Energy explains, "Since early recorded history, people have utilized wind energy."[6] The first recorded use of a windmill occurred in Mesopotamia, a region in present-day southwest Asia, in approximately 1700 BCE. These early machines were vertical-axis windmills, or windmills with blades that rotated around a vertical shaft. They converted the kinetic energy of wind into mechanical energy. Mechanical energy is the ability to do work. Windmills harnessed the power of wind to pump water, grind grains, and irrigate land. The wind spun a shaft, and the shaft connected to mechanical devices that would convert the rotational motion into motion useful for operating pumps and other machinery. Windmills were used for these purposes in Persia by 500 CE and in China by 1200 CE.

By the late 1300s CE, people in the Netherlands had also begun developing windmills. They built the first horizontal-axis windmills, called post mills, which consisted of four blades or sails that rotated around a shaft that was parallel to the ground. The Dutch used these windmills to drain waterlogged areas, which created new farmland. Windmills were later used throughout Europe to cut lumber in sawmills and to reduce wood pulp into paper.

Settlers in North America also used windmills to produce mechanical energy. The Wind Energy Foundation notes that they used windmills to "grind wheat and corn, to pump water and to cut wood at sawmills."[7]

By the mid-1800s, a new industry emerged that would lead to the development of the modern wind turbine. Inventors had realized the potential of electricity to power homes and cities. English scientist Michael Faraday discovered in 1831 that magnetism could produce electric currents in coils of wire. This later led to the development of generators, the devices that make it possible for wind turbines to produce electricity from the kinetic energy of wind.

Modern Wind Turbine Designs

Most wind turbines in use today are horizontal-axis wind turbines. In these turbines, the rotor turns around a horizontal shaft atop a tower. The nacelle in a horizontal-axis wind turbine is attached to the rotor. Horizontal-axis wind turbines can have one, two, or three blades. A three-blade configuration captures wind with the most efficiency. As scientist Dale E. Berg of Sandia National Laboratories puts it, "A combination of structural and economic considerations drives the use of three slender blades on most wind turbines."[8]

Vertical-axis wind turbines contain all of the same essential components as horizontal-axis wind turbines, but the configuration of their parts is different. Unlike the blades on horizontal-axis wind turbines, blades on vertical-axis wind turbines spin around a vertical shaft, perpendicular to the direction of airflow. The movement is similar to a carousel or merry-go-round. Vertical-axis wind turbines usually have two or three blades, and they are typically not as tall as horizontal-axis wind turbines. In a vertical-axis wind turbine, the gearbox is located at the base of the tower. Vertical-axis turbines do not require nacelles since the gearbox and the generator are located at the ground level.

The two main types of modern vertical-axis wind turbines are the Darrieus and the Savonius models. The Darrieus turbine contains two or three elongated blades that curve outward around a vertical shaft. Similar to the blades on horizontal-axis turbines, the blades on a Darrieus turbine use an airfoil design, using lift

Vertical-axis wind turbines are usually smaller than their horizontal-axis counterparts. However, they also have less power-generation capacity.

forces to turn the blades. As the blades spin, they look like a rotating eggbeater. The Darrieus windmill design was invented in France in the 1920s and received a US patent in 1931. The Savonius vertical-axis turbine consists of two or three scooped blades. The blades are attached to a vertical shaft, and they capture the wind like boat sails. The Savonius vertical-axis turbine was invented in Finland in 1922.

Vertical-axis turbines are designed so that they can capture wind from all directions. However, vertical-axis turbine blades move perpendicular to airflow, which is not an optimal angle to generate lift. Vertical-axis turbines are therefore not as efficient as horizontal-axis turbines.

Vertical-axis wind turbines are used in certain specific situations. They may be utilized on a small scale in areas where wind is not consistent or where laws limit the height of turbines. Finnish researcher Svetlana Marmutova notes that the "Savonius wind turbine can provide a good solution for wind power generation in cities due to its size and less sensitivity to the changes in wind speed and direction."[9] However, horizontal-axis turbines are generally preferred over vertical-axis turbines.

Efficiency and Capacity Factor

In order to determine how effective a wind turbine is, scientists measure its efficiency. Efficiency is a measurement that indicates how much of the kinetic energy from the wind is converted into electricity. Depending on the type of wind turbine and the wind conditions, wind turbines can convert between 12 and 50 percent of the wind passing through their blades into electricity. Utility-scale turbines that operate in areas with powerful winds might have efficiencies between 40 and 50 percent. Some energy is lost in the conversion process. Drag forces against the blades slow down the turbine. A turbine may also be stopped when the wind is blowing too fast. Slowing or stopping a turbine means it generates less power, decreasing its efficiency. Because of outside forces acting against a machine, no energy conversion system can operate at 100 percent efficiency.

Another important measurement related to a turbine's efficiency is its capacity factor. Capacity factor is a ratio of the actual power output of a turbine or wind farm over time compared with its maximum potential output. For example, if a wind turbine that has the potential to generate 5 megawatts per day instead generates on average 2 megawatts per day, then its capacity factor is 40 percent. A turbine's efficiency influences its capacity factor. Today, engineers are designing different types of turbines in an effort to increase efficiency and capacity factor.

Global Wind Power Potential

Some modern turbines have the potential to power entire towns or communities. In 2008, Rock Port, Missouri, became the first US town to be powered completely by wind. Four utility-scale wind turbines generate all of the electricity needed for the town's 1,300 residents. The installation harnesses the strong winds that sweep through the surrounding plains and prairies. University of Missouri engineer Jim Crawford compared the wind to the other crops in the region's farms: "We're farming the wind, which is something that we have up here. The payback on a per-acre basis is generally quite good when compared to a lot of other crops, and it's as simple as getting a cup of coffee and watching the blades spin."[10]

Farther south, more than 11,000 wind turbines dot the arid Texas landscape. Texas has more wind turbines and generates more electricity from wind than any other US state. Greg Wortham, chief executive officer for the Texas energy consulting firm New Amsterdam Global Solutions, assesses the impact the wind industry has had on Texas. "Wind came at exactly the right time and it fit the mentality of a lot of the folks that wanted green," Wortham said. "A lot of people were environmentalists or they wouldn't have held land, been stewards of land for a hundred years in the family. So they all cared but they didn't know how to activate that."[11] Today, many farmers and ranchers in Texas consider the leasing of their lands for wind turbine development a continuation of that same sense of **stewardship**.

Outside of the United States, many other countries are expanding the global wind power industry. According to the Global Wind Energy Council (GWEC), an association of wind energy experts, "More than 54 [gigawatts] of clean renewable wind power was installed across the global market in 2016, which now comprises more than 90 countries."[12] Altogether, wind turbines globally have the capacity to produce more than 480 gigawatts of electricity. Just 1 gigawatt of electricity has the potential to power more than 1 million homes.

China leads the way in wind power potential. More than 92,000 wind turbines have been installed across the country. In early 2017, the *New York Times* noted that "the government is adding them at a rate of more than one per hour."[13] China's wind turbines have the combined capacity to generate 145 gigawatts of electricity. However, China also burns more fossil fuels than any other country. China continues to rely heavily on coal as a source of energy. Nevertheless, many see the sizable installed capacity of China's wind turbines as a vital step in the right direction. In early 2017, GWEC secretary general

Steve Sawyer concluded: "We have a lot of confidence in the wind power market going forward, as the technology continues to improve, prices continue to go down and the call for clean, renewable power to reduce emissions, clean our air and create new jobs and new industries only gets stronger with each passing year."[14]

Measuring Power and Energy

When evaluating renewable energy sources, scientists study two main concepts with regard to electricity: power and energy. *Power* is a measurement of the rate at which electricity is transferred. Power is measured in watts. The greater the power, the more electricity is transferred at a certain time. For example, a 100-watt light bulb transfers more electricity per second than a 60-watt light bulb. *Energy* is a measurement of the total amount of electricity that is used over time. Energy is measured in watt-hours. For example, a 15-watt light bulb uses 15 watts of power at a specific moment in time. If it is turned on for one hour, it uses 15 watt-hours of energy.

Households typically require large amounts of power, measured in kilowatts. A kilowatt is equal to 1,000 watts. Even larger amounts of power are measured in megawatts or gigawatts. One megawatt is equal to 1 million watts. The power generated by a power plant is typically measured in megawatts. The power required for large cities or entire countries is measured in gigawatts. One gigawatt is equal to 1 billion watts. Large, utility-scale wind turbines can generate enough electricity to power an entire community, or thousands of households. The power generated by utility-scale wind turbines is usually measured in megawatts. Large turbines grouped into giant wind farms may collectively be able to generate enough power to be measured in gigawatts.

CAN WIND POWER
REPLACE FOSSIL FUELS?

While the global wind power industry has been expanding considerably in the last few decades, many countries around the world continue to rely heavily on fossil fuels as a source of energy. Fossil fuels are carbon-based materials that formed from prehistoric plants and animals. Millions of years ago, these organisms died and **decomposed**. Over time, this organic matter was compressed under layers of sediments such as rock, mud, or sand. The sediments shifted and accumulated, and the organic matter became buried hundreds or even thousands of feet underneath Earth's surface. The type of organism, the pressure and temperature during the decomposition process, and the length of time the material was buried all were factors that influenced the type of fossil fuel that developed.

> ## WORDS IN CONTEXT
> **decomposed**
> Broken down and decayed by natural processes.

Fossil fuels became increasingly in demand in the mid-1700s into the mid-1800s, during the Industrial Revolution in Britain and in the United States. Fossil fuels were extracted to power factories and machinery. The US Energy Information Administration (EIA) points out that "the three major fossil fuels—petroleum, natural gas, and coal—have dominated the US energy mix for more than 100 years."[15] These fossil fuels are used primarily to fuel vehicles, generate electricity, and heat homes and buildings.

The US Department of Energy notes that "coal is the most plentiful fuel in the fossil family and it has the longest and, perhaps, the most varied history."[16] Coal is a dense, brown or black material that formed from dead plants that lived millions of years ago. Layers of rock built up and buried these coal deposits. Coal mining became a major industry in Britain in the 1700s, and the coal mining industry in the United States took off in the 1740s. In coal mines, miners traveled deep into the Earth and extracted coal deposits. Coal was convenient because it was more abundant than other resources that could be used to generate heat, including firewood and charcoal. Coal burns slowly and releases energy in the form of heat as it burns.

New uses for coal were discovered in the mid-1800s during the peak period of the Industrial Revolution. Coal was burned in a furnace, heating water that ran through tubes inside the furnace. The water became steam, and the steam turned a turbine to produce electricity. While coal was used to generate electricity for homes and factories in this way in the late 1800s, it also fueled steam engines on railroads.

Coal power plants create severe pollution. Many countries are beginning to phase them out in favor of cleaner energy sources.

Today, coal is mainly used to generate electricity. Most of the world's coal reserves are located in Europe and in North America. Coal currently generates approximately half of the electricity in the United States. Coal is also used to manufacture steel.

Many countries also rely on oil, another common fossil fuel. It is a thick liquid found underground. It was formed millions of years ago as prehistoric organisms were compressed under river and ocean sediments. The first oil well was drilled in Pennsylvania in 1859. In the late 1800s, automobiles fueled by gasoline were invented. Gasoline is made from oil that has been **refined**. Today, consumers continue to use oil, typically in the form of gasoline or diesel fuel, to power vehicles. The EIA calculated that "in 2016, about 143.37 billion gallons (542.71 billion L) of finished motor gasoline were consumed in the United States. . . . This was the largest amount of annual motor gasoline consumption on record."[17] However, oil does have other widespread uses. Oil is also used to generate heat and electricity, and refined oil is commonly used to make products such as asphalt and plastic. As of 2016, oil was consumed worldwide at a rate of approximately 96 million barrels each day. One barrel of oil is equal to 42 gallons (159 L).

Natural gas is another commonly used fossil fuel worldwide. The same prehistoric geological processes that created oil also created natural gas. Natural gas is an odorless and colorless gas made up primarily of a chemical called methane. Methane consists of carbon and hydrogen, and it is highly flammable. Natural gas passed through pores in rocks, but some got trapped under layers of rocks underground. Buried deep beneath Earth's surface, it formed natural gas deposits. Natural gas is also commonly found dissolved in oil deposits.

A lack of adequate, long-distance pipe systems prevented the widespread use of natural gas until the 1900s. Such pipeline transmission systems were constructed in some countries in the 1930s and 1940s, but natural gas did not become a major energy source until a few decades later. Today, many power plants use natural gas to generate electricity. Consumers also use natural gas for cooking, lighting, and heating.

The major sectors of the modern energy market continue to be coal, oil, and natural gas. Among industrially developed countries, including the United States, fossil fuels supply more than 80 percent of the energy demand. As of 2016, coal, oil, and natural gas accounted for more than 60 percent of the electricity generated in the United States. In that same year, wind energy accounted for a mere 5.6 percent of the electricity generated in the United States.

Fossil fuels continue to dominate the global energy market for a number of reasons. Fossil fuels have the advantage of being the more well-established energy source over renewable energy sources, including wind energy. Onshore wind turbine development for commercial use did not become widespread until the 1970s, when political conflicts in the Middle East—a region that contains vast oil reserves—limited many countries' access to oil. Offshore wind is an even younger sector of the wind energy market, as offshore wind projects weren't developed for commercial use until the 1990s. Since people have widely used fossil fuels for hundreds of years, many energy experts are more familiar with fossil fuels than with lesser-used renewable sources of electricity, including wind. Fossil fuels are also dense materials that contain great amounts of energy within a small mass or volume. Their compact nature additionally makes them easier and cheaper to transport than the large equipment necessary for wind turbines.

Despite the advantages fossil fuels present over wind energy, the wind power industry continues to expand globally each year. Wind power has some key advantages over fossil fuels, leading to a greater global push for wind power development over the last few decades. The availability of tax credits and supportive government policies will likely also continue to shape the future of wind energy.

Fossil Fuel Problems and Wind Benefits

Fossil fuels have continually been relied upon as a primary source of energy worldwide because they have some established advantages over renewable resources. However, new wind energy technologies and the growth and success of the wind power industry have helped close this gap. Furthermore, fossil fuels have significant disadvantages that make renewable energy sources such as wind more beneficial from environmental, public health, and economic perspectives.

One key problem associated with fossil fuels is their emission of greenhouse gases. As carbon-dense fossil fuels are burned, they release carbon dioxide and other gases into the atmosphere. Some carbon dioxide exists naturally in Earth's atmosphere. As animals breathe, organic matter decomposes, volcanoes erupt, and natural forest fires occur, carbon dioxide is released into the atmosphere. However, additional carbon dioxide emitted from burning fossil fuels contributes to the greenhouse effect. This phenomenon occurs when water vapor, carbon dioxide, methane, and other gases referred to as greenhouse gases collect in the lowest layer of Earth's atmosphere.

Most of the light from the Sun passes through Earth's atmosphere and reaches the planet's surface. But part of this energy is reflected back toward space as **infrared radiation**. Greenhouse gases absorb and contain this radiation. This raises the temperature of Earth's atmosphere.

WORDS IN CONTEXT

infrared radiation
A type of energy that is radiated, or emitted, as heat.

The greenhouse effect is a natural phenomenon that plays an important role in making Earth livable. If greenhouse gases were entirely absent from Earth's atmosphere and there were no greenhouse effect, the planet's surface temperature would only reach about 0°F (–18°C). However, most scientists have concluded that the burning of fossil fuels is accelerating the greenhouse effect. The concentration of carbon dioxide in Earth's atmosphere was first measured in 1958. At that time, scientists measured the carbon dioxide concentration at 317 parts per million (ppm). By 2013, however, carbon dioxide concentration had exceeded 400 ppm. As the carbon dioxide concentration increases, average global temperatures rise. The average global temperature over both land and ocean surfaces in 2017 was about 1.6°F (0.9°C) higher than the average global temperature measured in the 1900s. At this rate of warming, some scientists estimate that the average global temperature may increase by approximately 4.9°F (2.7°C) by the year 2100. Such an increase may not seem like much, but it could have long-term, far-reaching effects. Sea levels would rise as glaciers continue to melt. Since hurricanes form over warm ocean waters, these tropical storms may become more frequent and intense. Rising tides and powerful hurricanes could damage coastal communities. Longer periods of droughts and heat waves could lead to water shortages and affect rural farming economies. Rising temperatures could also make precipitation patterns more variable and more difficult to predict, which could damage crops or alter growing seasons. Rising temperatures would thus affect the weather of many regions in addition to Earth's overall climate. Weather differs from climate. NASA explains, "The difference between weather and climate is a measure of time. Weather is what conditions of the atmosphere are over a short period of time, and climate is how the atmosphere 'behaves' over relatively long periods of time."[18] Because rising temperatures would alter the planet's climate, this effect is referred to as climate change.

While many scientists who study climate change believe its effects cannot be reversed, most see renewable energies as a key to at least slowing these effects. Wind turbines harness energy without emitting greenhouse gases. The turbine manufacturing and construction processes do release fossil fuels, however. The materials used to make wind turbines typically include concrete, steel, and fiberglass. Steel is usually made from iron ore, and the equipment required to mine iron ore runs on diesel fuel. Furnaces help shape the iron ore and melt glass that is used in turbines, and these furnaces are often powered by coal. Cement is used to make concrete, and cement is mixed in a kiln, which runs on coal or natural gas. Carbon dioxide is a by-product of the chemical reaction needed to make cement. Additionally, machines such as trucks and cranes that transport these

Unlike fossil fuels, wind is a resource that is freely available to anyone. Each turbine covers a relatively small footprint of land.

materials run on diesel fuel. An oil product called lubricant is used in a turbine's gearboxes to help the gears turn easily. However, if a wind turbine is placed in a windy area and its design makes it efficient, the clean energy generated by the turbine offsets the greenhouse gases used to build it. The average modern wind turbine has the capacity to produce 2 megawatts of electricity and avoids more than 2,000 tons (1,800 metric t) of carbon dioxide emissions per year.

In addition to the negative environmental effects of fossil fuels, another disadvantage of these resources is that they are not renewable. Although fossil fuels have historically been plentiful in many places throughout the world, their availability becomes limited as people continue to extract them. Scientists predict that fossil fuel production will naturally decline within the next few decades as supplies dwindle and reserves become increasingly difficult to find. In contrast, wind is an abundant and inexhaustible supply of energy. Access to wind, unlike access to fossil fuels, is free.

Fossil fuel extraction is not only harmful to the environment but also often detrimental to the health of workers and the general public. Coal miners may suffer health problems as a result of breathing in coal dust over long periods of time. The most common health problem resulting from this is black lung disease, which affects a miner's respiratory system and ability to breathe properly. Hazardous accidents can also occur in coal mines. The roof of a coal mine may collapse, which can trap or crush miners. As flammable gases are released during the mining process, another danger posed to miners is the risk of fire or explosions. And as miners are exposed to dangers within the mine, people who live nearby are exposed to pollutants from the coal production process. The burning of coal also releases gases that bind with moisture in the atmosphere to produce **acid rain**. Acid rain is rain with a high acidity, which damages plants.

Oil extraction and transportation can also be hazardous. Oil is transported in mass quantities via large ships called tankers. Oil can spill if tankers run aground. This type of incident occurred with disastrous consequences when the *Exxon Valdez* tanker crashed into a reef in the Gulf of Alaska in 1989. Offshore oil rigs can also explode, causing oil to spill into the sea. The Deepwater Horizon rig in the Gulf of Mexico exploded in 2010, resulting in the largest marine oil spill in history. Both this event and the *Exxon Valdez* oil spill polluted seas, harmed wildlife, and damaged the fishing industry. Such disasters have long-lasting consequences. A few years after the Deepwater Horizon spill, Kara Lankford of the Ocean Conservancy, an environmental group, said, "The . . . oil disaster may not be on the national radar as much as it was four (almost five) years ago; however, in the minds of Gulf residents it is never forgotten. We are reminded of this disaster when a storm washes tar balls on the beach, or when scientific studies are released that point to injury of the ecosystem."[19]

In contrast to the fossil fuel industry, the wind energy industry generally offers safer environments for its workers. The job of a wind turbine technician is the most dangerous one in the industry. Technicians who repair turbine components have to regularly climb high turbine towers, since much of a turbine's equipment is located at the top of its tower within the nacelle. However, safety rules help protect technicians. They receive extensive training for their work, and when climbing towers they use lanyard ropes to anchor them to the structure.

As fossil fuel supplies dwindle, renewable energy industries are expected to expand to meet the world's energy demands. Within the United States, the rate of job growth in the renewable energy sector is outpacing the rate of job growth in the fossil fuel industry. By 2016, the number of people employed in the US wind industry surpassed 100,000. In that same year, the number of jobs created by the global wind turbine industry surpassed 1.1 million. As of 2016, wind turbine technician was the fastest-growing occupation in the United States, and it was estimated that the number of wind turbine technicians would double in the next decade as the country planned more wind turbine projects. While the number of fossil fuel jobs worldwide and in the United States still exceeds the number of wind industry jobs, the recent expansion of the wind industry is a strong indicator it will continue to grow.

Wind Challenges—Technical

Although wind energy has many distinct advantages over fossil fuels, it does come with some drawbacks. When scientists and energy experts assess the potential of wind power or other renewable energies to replace fossil fuels, they take into consideration not only the disadvantages of fossil fuels but the disadvantages of the renewable energy source.

One of the biggest challenges the wind industry faces is the intermittent nature of wind. Wind speed can vary considerably within a 24-hour period, which means that relying on wind turbines for consistent electricity generation may not always be possible. The electricity wind turbines generate may exceed energy demands when winds are strong or fall short during lull periods when wind speeds are slow. Wind energy researchers and scientists are working on possible solutions to this problem. One way that the US Department of Energy's National Renewable Energy Laboratory has suggested this can be addressed in the United States is by distributing more wind turbines all across the country and linking them into a common power grid. Since winds blow at varying speeds in different places and at different times, a turbine system spread across a larger area would be able to capture wind power more consistently than a localized turbine system. Another solution to this problem involves storing surplus electricity generated by wind turbines in batteries. The stored electricity in batteries can then be used when the wind stops blowing. Researchers are developing other storage systems that use the electricity from wind turbines to compress air. The air is stored in underground caves. When more electricity is needed, some of the compressed air is released, driving a turbine to generate power. One such project is in Houston, Texas. The *Houston Chronicle* wrote, "Texans have long stored oil, natural gas and other forms of energy in underground salt caverns, so it's only natural that a Houston startup wants to store wind energy there, too."[20]

Another common technical problem with wind turbines is that they are often built in rural areas, away from cities and major population centers. Buildings and other man-made obstacles obstruct the path of wind. Wind is therefore usually strongest in flat, open fields, which are more common in rural areas. But electrical demand is higher in cities

Wind turbines must be paired with electricity transmission systems to get the power to places where it is needed. These systems can be complex and expensive.

than in rural areas. Building long transmission lines to connect wind turbines in remote areas to a city's electrical grid can be costly and labor-intensive.

In addition to these issues, feeding wind turbine transmission lines into an existing electrical grid can place strain on the grid. Cables in a power grid can handle a certain amount of voltage. If the voltage output exceeds the amount that the grid can handle, power outages and damage to the grid can result. In the United States, the existing electrical grid system is aging and increasingly subject to power outages. It was not designed to handle modern electricity demands. Otto J. Lynch is the vice president of Power Line Systems, a US company that helps design power transmission lines. He explains:

> I like to think of our grid much like a water system, and
> basically all of our pipes are at full pressure now. . . . If one
> of our pipes bursts and we have to shut off that line, that just
> increases the pressure on our remaining pipes until another
> one bursts, and next thing you know, we're in a catastrophic
> run and we have to shut the whole water system down.[21]

Upgrades to the US electrical grid are in progress, and developing power plants that will be better able to work in conjunction with wind farms will help balance the electrical outputs of wind energy with conventional sources.

Wind Challenges—Environment

While wind turbines generate electricity without emitting greenhouse gases, some conservationists and wildlife biologists have raised questions about turbines' effects on wildlife. A 2013 study conducted by scientists from the US Fish and Wildlife Service and the Smithsonian Conservation Biology Institute found that "wind turbines kill an estimated 140,000 to 328,000 birds each year in North America."[22] Bird casualties are highest when turbines are built near a bird's habitat, within a migrating species' flight path, or within an area that has a high concentration of prey animals. Many times, birds cannot see turbine blades as they spin due to a phenomenon called motion smear. Blade tip speeds usually range from 138 to 182 miles

Altamont Pass Wind Farm

Golden eagles are vulnerable to turbine collisions in California. While these birds are common in western states, they are listed as endangered in some eastern states. A particular area of concern was Altamont, California, where one wind farm has historically killed more than 75 golden eagles each year. Many of the turbines in the wind farm, called Altamont Pass Wind Farm, were built in the 1970s. Older wind turbines are typically smaller than modern wind turbines, and wind farms with smaller turbines require more of them to capture the same amount of energy as wind farms with larger turbines. Many small turbines can mean more bird deaths than fewer larger ones. At peak development of the Altamont Pass Wind Farm in the 1990s, 7,000 turbines were in operation. The turbines were built on or near the habitats of animals that are common prey for the golden eagle, and collisions commonly occurred as golden eagles dove to catch prey.

After researchers discovered the number of golden eagle deaths at the Altamont Pass Wind Farm, the farm closed in 2015. The outdated turbines will be replaced by a smaller wind farm with modern turbines, which is expected to reduce the rate of bird collisions in the area. Additionally, the National Wind Technology Center in Boulder, Colorado, is funding a number of projects, including advanced camera detection systems that could be mounted on turbines. These technological solutions might help reduce the rate of eagle collisions.

per hour (222 to 293 km/h), and at this speed, individual blades become harder to identify.

Songbirds are the species most affected by wind turbine development. In general, songbirds are vulnerable to collisions with many human-made structures, including buildings, power transmission lines, vehicles, and communication towers. Compared with the songbird mortality rates from collisions with other human-made structures, the mortality rate from collision with wind turbines is relatively low.

Wind turbines also sometimes affect bats. Bats use sonar navigation at night and are therefore better able to detect turbine blades than birds. However, bats cannot detect the areas of low pressure that form behind spinning turbine blades. When bats fly into this wake, or **vortex**, the pressure difference causes their internal airways to expand. This leads to internal bleeding, which often kills bats.

Turbine manufacturing companies have developed some ways to reduce avian fatalities, and they continue to work on more ways to increase safety for birds and bats. Studies have shown that purple-colored wind turbines may be effective at deterring birds and bats. Insects that birds and bats feed on are attracted to white or muted colors, and most turbines are painted in these colors. The color purple seems to be the least attractive to insects. Another study has found that **ultraviolet** lighting systems installed alongside turbines could be effective at deterring birds and bats. Besides technological developments, other common solutions that modern turbine developers consider include constructing new turbines in areas that are farther away from bird and bat habitats and are not in bird migration paths.

Wind Energy Policies and Incentives

Another key factor that will help determine whether it is feasible to replace fossil fuels with wind power is government policies and incentives. Local and national governments have the ability to support or hinder the development of the wind industry. Current policies in place in many countries support the wind industry. In many cases, the government offers tax credits or **subsidies** to turbine developers. The upfront costs associated with turbine development can be significant. In addition to the cost of the turbine itself, developers must factor in the cost of permits,

installation, construction, and operating costs. Wind turbines can operate for 20 years or more after they are connected to the grid, and they require maintenance from wind technicians and operators. The capacity factor of a turbine also affects costs. Taller wind towers in areas with strong winds are likely to be the most efficient, although larger turbines typically require greater upfront **investment** costs. Government tax credits and subsidies can assist with these costs. Tax credits are deductions from the amount of taxes owed by wind turbine operators. Typically, large turbines that produce a great deal of energy receive the most tax credits. However, small, residential wind turbines can also receive federal tax credits. Tax credits for residential wind turbines can cover installation costs.

In 1992, the Production Tax Credit (PTC) was implemented in the United States as a part of the Energy Policy Act. The PTC has been renewed and expanded several times since it was first put in place in 1992. It provided a tax credit of 2.3 cents per kilowatt-hour in 2015 for utility-scale wind turbines that produce electricity. This tax credit amount is adjusted for inflation. The House of Representatives and the Senate agreed to extend the PTC in 2015, but the tax credit will again expire in 2020. While this federal tax credit has proven beneficial to utility-scale turbine developers, its survival depends on government officials who may or may not choose to continue renewing it in the future. Iowa senator Chuck Grassley, who helped create the credit, explained why he believed it was so important: "We knew it had environmental benefits that were very important, but I would say making sure we were more energy independent was the most important reason for supporting all forms of alternative energy."[23]

Replacing Fossil Fuels

Technical, environmental, and policy issues are the major concerns to be considered when assessing whether wind power may eventually replace fossil fuels. While fossil fuels have many of their own serious disadvantages, people around the world have utilized fossil fuels as an energy source for centuries. Because of this strong global dependence on fossil fuels, many people are skeptical of wind power's potential to outpace the growth of the fossil fuel industry. Certainly, steps toward phasing out fossil fuels in favor of renewable energy do face some significant challenges. However, some analysts predict that renewable energy, including wind power, could replace fossil fuels in the future if adequate measures are taken to continue reducing fossil fuel use. In 2015, the GWEC and the nonprofit environmental organization Greenpeace International published a report that concluded that renewable energy sources could replace fossil fuels by 2050. Scientist Sven Teske, the lead author of the report, said:

> Wind and solar technologies are mainstream now, and are cost-competitive with coal today. It is very likely that they will overtake the coal industry in terms of jobs and energy supplied within the next decade.[24]

HOW DOES OFFSHORE COMPARE WITH ONSHORE WIND?

O nshore and offshore wind systems have both expanded in the last few decades. However, global onshore wind development continues to grow at a faster rate than global offshore wind development. While offshore turbines are able to harness stronger winds that sweep unobstructed across seas and oceans, they are also typically more labor-intensive and costly to install. Onshore wind systems have traditionally dominated the wind energy market. But as offshore wind costs drop, offshore development is becoming increasingly attractive. Developing both types of systems has strengthened the wind industry. Onshore and offshore wind systems have proven to be increasingly competitive against established energy sources such as fossil fuels. Furthermore, many developers are becoming more aware of the broader benefits of offshore wind development and the ways in which offshore and onshore wind farms can complement each other. In this way, researchers and

The V164 turbines dwarf the ships that arrive to maintain them. Thanks to their size, they generate enormous amounts of power.

energy experts predict that advances in both offshore and onshore technology will shape the future of the global wind industry.

Offshore Wind Developments

On May 17, 2017, strong winds swept off the west coast of England in Liverpool Bay. The gusts spun the blades of 32 massive MHI Vestas V164 turbines. The turbine towers rose about 640 feet (195 m) above the water. The turbine blades were each 262 feet (80 m) long, the equivalent of nine double-decker London buses stacked end-to-end. At the time of its development, the MHI Vestas V164 turbine was the largest wind turbine in the world. These 32 state-of-the-art turbines added 258 megawatts of power to the existing Burbo Bank Wind

Farm, enough to supply electricity to more than 230,000 homes at peak periods of operation.

The success of the Burbo Bank Extension demonstrated clearly the singular benefits of offshore wind and the technological advancements that have been made in the offshore wind market. Dong Energy, the Danish offshore wind developer that installed Vindeby, the world's first offshore wind farm, led the development of the Burbo Bank Extension. MHI Vestas Offshore Wind company engineered and manufactured the turbines' components. Dong Energy has said that just one V164 turbine has the capacity to generate more energy than the entirety of the former Vindeby Wind Farm, which was developed in 1991. These new turbines also each can generate more than twice the power of the neighboring turbines in the original Burbo Bank Wind Farm, which was installed about a decade earlier. A single **revolution** of one of these turbines' blades can produce enough electricity to power one home for 29 hours.

A local manager for Dong Energy noted that gaining experience in developing offshore wind power can help bring costs down for everyone: "This and other projects have been crucial for driving costs down for the whole industry."[25]

Modern turbine models like the V164 have shaped the future of the offshore wind industry. These large turbines have reduced the costs of offshore wind development due in part to their size. Each turbine that is anchored to the seafloor requires a foundation and a support system in addition to cables to connect it to a substation. Furthermore, each offshore turbine requires maintenance, and maintenance of offshore turbines is an important factor in an offshore wind farm's overall cost. When turbines are larger and more efficient, fewer of them are required in order to meet power needs. Offshore wind farms that are smaller in size require less maintenance.

As with onshore turbines, the size of an offshore turbine affects its power output and efficiency. Taller offshore turbines are able to generate more power because winds are stronger at higher altitudes. Across the seas that border Europe, wind speeds can reach 22 miles per hour (35 km/h) at a height of 360 feet (110 m) above the surface. This is nearly three times the average onshore wind speed. In the early years of offshore wind development, the standard offshore turbine was not tall enough to access these stronger wind speeds. Early offshore turbine models developed in the late 1990s and early 2000s had a height of approximately 210 feet (64 m) and a nameplate capacity of 1 to 2 megawatts. The term *nameplate capacity* indicates the maximum power output of a turbine's generator under optimal conditions and wind speeds, typically between 30 and 50 miles per hour (48 to 80 km/h). As developers designed larger offshore turbines, nameplate capacities increased. The V164 has a nameplate capacity of 8 megawatts. Within the next decade, standard offshore turbine models will likely increase even more in size and may have a nameplate capacity of 13 to 15 megawatts. The company behind the V164 is confident that its technology will help push the industry forward: "We believe that our wind turbine will play an integral part in enabling the offshore industry to continue to drive down the cost of energy."[26]

More energy companies, including even some multinational oil and gas companies such as Royal Dutch Shell and Statoil ASA, are investing in offshore wind as it increasingly becomes a more attractive and reliable energy source. Following the success of Block Island Wind Farm, the United States is also poised to develop more offshore wind projects in the near future. Most of the nation's electricity demands lie in coastal states and along the Great Lakes, so offshore wind developments would be most advantageous for residents living in these areas. If such projects are realized in the near future, offshore wind will make even greater contributions to the growth of the global wind industry.

Offshore Challenges—Installation and Maintenance

While offshore wind costs have been falling drastically in the past few years, the *Guardian* newspaper notes that onshore wind generation is "around half the cost of offshore wind and a quarter of the costs of solar photovoltaic panels."[27] Much of this added cost comes from installation and maintenance challenges that arise from developing infrastructure in seas and oceans. Though offshore turbines have all the same components as onshore turbines, they are typically larger, and they also require support system equipment to anchor them

Offshore wind installations require huge vessels with massive cranes. This is one of many challenges facing offshore wind development.

to the bottom of a sea or an ocean. Transporting, installing, and maintaining these components in large bodies of water can be difficult and expensive.

The first structure that is installed for an offshore wind project is typically a meteorological mast, also called a met tower. A met tower is not a component of an offshore wind turbine, but it collects critical weather data that help developers and engineers plan offshore wind projects. A met tower contains sensors that measure wind speed, wind direction, the velocity of ocean or sea currents, and water temperature. This information helps developers estimate power output and estimate how much it will cost to maintain the turbines. Offshore wind developer Paul Rich described the importance of a met tower on a project he worked on: "This is an important step in understanding the logistics of the project. This will really help us understand the scale of the wind out at sea."[28]

Offshore turbine components are constructed and assembled in onshore factories. The first of these components is the foundation. An offshore turbine's foundation is the structural support that anchors it to a seafloor. Factors such as wind speed, wave height, and water depth influence the type and design of a foundation. The transition piece is a tube that connects the foundation to the turbine tower. It contains platforms, ladders, and boat landings, which give workers access to turbines for maintenance purposes. A crane on a barge or vessel lifts and installs the transition piece. External or internal tubes called J-tubes are also a part of the transition piece. These tubes house cables that transmit electrical power from the turbine to a substation. Many of the cables are buried underground, in the seafloor. The cables connect turbines within an **array** to each other and to the substation, and the substation in turn transmits the electrical current to an onshore power grid. Substations may be located onshore or offshore in shallow waters so that they are closer to the turbines.

After all of these support system parts have been installed, cranes lift the turbine components—the tower, nacelle, and rotor—onto a jack-up vessel that is equipped to carry these massive loads. Once it reaches the installation site, the jack-up vessel is able to rise up on footings about 60 feet (18 m) above the water. This provides a safe, steady platform for workers that is high above any dangerous,

turbulent waves. A crane on the vessel lifts and installs the tower atop the transition piece. The crane also lifts and places the nacelle with the turbine's generator and the blades. Workers bolt the

equipment together. This main part of the installation process may take anywhere between one and seven days, depending on the type of turbine as well as the weather and installation conditions.

One common problem that can occur with offshore turbines is corrosion. Corrosion happens when salt water eats away at metal. Turbine components are coated in materials such as zinc and aluminum, which are supposed to keep oxygen and water from reaching the metal structure underneath. Grout and other strong sealants are used to prevent leaks. Still, water leaks can occur, which can cause corrosion inside and outside the turbine's tower. Though offshore turbines are built using strong materials such as fiberglass, heavy storms at sea and drifting sea ice have the potential to damage these turbines. Additionally, storms can affect workers' access to turbines and may delay maintenance. When maintenance is delayed, some offshore power production is lost.

Engineers continue to develop ways to improve the strength and endurance of offshore turbines. Some scientists are developing turbine blades with stronger but lighter materials, such as polyurethane reinforced with nanotubes. Polyurethane is a hard, sturdy plastic material. Nanotubes are microscopic, tube-shaped structures made of carbon. Studies have shown that nanotube-reinforced polyurethane blades are substantially stronger, lighter, and more rigid than fiberglass. These better-performing blade materials could have applications for both onshore and offshore turbines. They could allow engineers to make even longer turbine blades. As turbine blade length

Hornsea Wind Farm

While offshore maintenance crews currently ferry back and forth from the mainland to offshore turbines, new projects under development may allow workers to remain out at sea for longer periods of time. One such project is the Hornsea Wind Farm, which Dong Energy plans to build in the North Sea, approximately 75 miles (121 km) off of England's northeast coast. The large wind farm will be built in three phases. The first phase of the project, called Hornsea Project One, is slated for completion in 2021. Dong Energy predicts that the entire wind farm will be completed in the mid-2020s. Each turbine in the Hornsea Wind Farm will be 623 feet (190 m) tall and will be capable of producing 7 megawatts of electricity. Once connected to the power grid, Hornsea Wind Farm might be capable of generating between 4 and 6 gigawatts of electricity. That would be enough electricity to power to more than 4 million households, or about 15 percent of all households in the United Kingdom. This would make the Hornsea Wind Farm the largest offshore wind farm in the world. In order to maintain such a massive wind farm, large maintenance crews and technicians are needed. The Hornsea Wind Farm will be equipped with two jack-up vessels, which will have the capacity to support as many as 150 technicians. These vessels will allow technicians to comfortably wait out storms at sea. In 2016, an official with Dong Energy stated, "Almost a decade on from initial planning, and following years of vital development work from a number of different companies in the supply chain, we are now ready to build the world's largest offshore wind farm."

Quoted in "World's Largest Ever Offshore Wind Farm to Be Built by Dong Energy," *Dong Energy*, February 3, 2016. www.dongenergy.co.uk.

increases, the radius of the **swept area** increases, which means that longer blades are able to harness more wind power and generate more electricity.

WORDS IN CONTEXT

swept area
The area of the circle that is created when a turbine's blades spin; the greater a turbine's swept area, the more winds its blades will capture.

In 2017, researchers from the University of Colorado Boulder conducted simulations to determine how a Category 5 hurricane, the strongest and most devastating category of hurricane, would affect modern wind turbine designs. While offshore turbines have never been tested by Category 5 hurricanes in real life, typhoons that hit the coasts of Japan and China in 2003 damaged several offshore turbines. The researchers noted, "We hope that this research will aid wind turbine manufacturers and developers in successfully tapping into the incredibly powerful wind resource just beyond our coastlines."[29] As US developers consider offshore projects in hurricane-prone regions such as the Gulf of Mexico and the Atlantic Ocean, such studies may prove to be especially helpful.

Offshore Wind and the Environment

As offshore wind power continues to be developed, a common concern expressed by some biologists and by the general public is that offshore turbines might have negative effects on the environment. Tom Miller of the University of Maryland points out that studying such effects is an important part of wind energy installations: "A critical element of wind energy planning is developing projects in such a way that we avoid or minimize negative environmental impacts those installations may cause."[30] Since offshore turbines operate in seas and oceans, their effects on marine wildlife in addition to their effects on birds are at the center of this discussion. Many of the most extensive studies on this subject have been conducted only recently, in the early 2000s. More research is needed to tell whether there might be other negative effects on the environment. However, studies thus far have generally indicated that offshore turbines have a neutral or, in some cases, even a positive effect on local wildlife.

Onshore turbines have been criticized for their effects on birds and bats. However, offshore turbines have typically not been subject to the same criticisms. This is because studies have shown that offshore turbines do not have the same impact on birds as onshore turbines. Bird populations are significantly lower in offshore environments than they are on land. Seabirds and waterfowl soar over seas and oceans, but they fly at **altitudes** below the swept areas of turbine blades. Migrating bird species tend to fly above the turbines. There have been some bird fatalities due to offshore turbines, but collision rates have been minimal in comparison with the natural mortality rate. Additionally, studies have found that offshore turbines also have negligible to no effect on bats. Though a few bat species migrate offshore, most remain on land. Bats that migrate offshore tend to fly at altitudes below the swept areas of turbine blades.

Environmental studies have also assessed the effects of offshore wind turbines on marine wildlife at all stages in the process—from installation to operation. Miller explains, "Making these decisions requires a year-round understanding of the species that frequent the area, particularly for protected species that are sensitive to sound, such as marine mammals."[31] As offshore wind development expanded in Europe, some conservationists became particularly concerned about the effects of offshore projects on harbor porpoises, a species of sea mammal that is related to dolphins. Harbor porpoises inhabit coastal waters in the Northern Hemisphere, including the North Sea. The fishing industry has depleted their prey resources, and chemical pollution has destroyed some of their habitat. Because harbor porpoises have been particularly vulnerable to human activity in these ways, researchers wanted to investigate whether offshore turbine developments would similarly have negative effects on this species.

From 2008 to 2010, scientists from Germany and the Netherlands surveyed the effects of offshore turbine installations on harbor porpoises in the North Sea. They discovered that the installation activities disrupted harbor porpoise behavior, causing them to avoid installation sites in the short term. After construction had concluded, however, harbor porpoise activity resumed in the area as normal. Additionally, an earlier study in the North Sea had measured greater harbor porpoise activity in the area during normal wind farm operations. The study hypothesized that harbor porpoises might be attracted to offshore wind structures because the structures provided shelter from boat traffic or else due to a reef effect. A reef

Harbor porpoises are among the species that can be affected by offshore turbines. Scientists track the animals' movements to study the turbines' impact.

effect occurs when crustaceans, underwater plants, and fish that one might find in a natural reef environment cluster on the foundations of the turbines. Impact assessments have shown that offshore wind operations have little effect on local wildlife compared with other methods of power generation. Because of this, the National Wildlife Federation (NWF) recommends the continued expansion of offshore wind. After Block Island Wind Farm was completed in 2017, the NWF sponsored a boat tour of the new offshore turbines. Matthew Morrissey of Deepwater Wind, the developer of the project, commented:

> This kind of (boat) trip allows our company to talk about how offshore wind can be built and has been built in the United States. It's an opportunity to come together and see that you can actually build a new economy in America while protecting the environment.[32]

Wind Power in the Developing World

While developed countries are increasingly looking to expand offshore wind power, offshore developments are often not feasible in other parts of the world. Offshore wind is still significantly more expensive than onshore wind, and some poor countries lack the economic resources to invest in it. Further complicating matters, reliable electrical grids are scarce in some developing countries. Some developing countries, such as India, have power grids that are aging and subject to power outages.

New and emerging technologies, in addition to increased global demands for electricity and alternative energy solutions, promise to make both onshore and offshore wind more affordable in the future. Abundant wind resources in many parts of the world, including developed and developing countries, make wind power an attractive and competitive energy source. Cost constraints may continue to make offshore wind less feasible than onshore wind in developing countries. But as the cost of offshore wind is projected to drop, it may become a more cost-effective option in the foreseeable future. Both onshore and offshore wind have disadvantages, but these can be managed as both forms of wind power are developed around the world. Writing about renewable energy sources, a report by Bloomberg New Energy Finance noted, "These technologies are poised to make an immediate impact on energy supply and access in the developing world."[33]

WHAT IS THE FUTURE OF WIND POWER?

As modern wind turbines harness energy on land and in seas and oceans, engineers continue to explore new frontiers and applications for wind power. Some are building floating turbines that can capture stronger winds in deep waters, farther from coasts. Others are developing airborne turbines that could harness stronger and more reliable winds at greater heights. Additional technological developments aim to increase the durability and efficiency of wind turbines. New designs under consideration by some energy companies may reduce the bird collision rates of onshore turbines. Many of these technological advancements have the potential to drive down the cost of wind power and make the wind industry more competitive with other energy sources.

Floating Turbines

Offshore wind farms have sprung up in Europe's North Sea because it is an ideal location for offshore development. Traditional, fixed-bottom offshore turbines require locations with depths of 65 to 164 feet (20 to

50 m) so that the foundations remain stable. The North Sea has uniquely shallow waters that make it attractive to offshore wind developers. But many of the coastal areas around the world have waters too deep for fixed-bottom offshore turbines. In order to develop offshore projects in these areas and harness stronger and steadier winds farther from the coasts, a new turbine design is necessary. For these purposes, manufacturers are experimenting with floating turbines. Anchors and thick cables moor the turbines to the seafloor, and buoys stabilize them. Engineer Andy Thompson explains, "Floating wind [turbines are] there to make the most of high winds and more reliable wind and that generally happens in deeper waters."[34]

Floating turbines enable power companies to use deeper waters. Stronger winds are often available in these areas.

In 2017, Norwegian energy company Statoil began transporting five floating turbines across the North Sea to a location off the coast of northeast Scotland. This wind farm, called Hywind Scotland, would be the world's first floating wind farm. The turbines had been assembled off the coast of Norway and tested for six years in the

North Sea. Vessels later towed the turbines to their final destination in Scottish waters. Scotland's deputy first minister, John Swinney, views the Hywind project as promising for Scotland's economy and, more broadly, for the growth of the global wind industry. He says:

> The momentum is building around the potential for floating offshore wind technology to unlock deeper water sites. The ability to leverage existing infrastructure and supply chain capabilities from the offshore oil and gas industry [creates] the ideal conditions to position Scotland as a world leader in floating wind technology.[35]

Expectations for floating turbines are high. Stephan Barth of IEA Wind, an international wind energy group, believes that the future of this technology is especially bright. He says, "Looking to the next decades, there might be a point where floating is bigger than fixed based."[36]

Airborne Alternatives—Kite Systems

As manufacturers build ever taller and bigger wind turbines, others are experimenting with more innovative ways to capture strong winds at high altitudes. **Wind power density**, which is a measurement of the amount of wind energy available at a given location, is greatest at approximately 32,000 feet (9,754 m) above

Earth's surface. Most airborne turbines in development can operate at heights of 1,000 to 2,000 feet (305 to 610 m), where winds are about five to eight times more powerful than winds near Earth's surface. Technology companies around the world are working on airborne turbines that operate like kites. Makani, a division of the technology company Google, is currently developing airborne turbines. The company's website explains the advantage of this technology: "By using a flexible tether instead of a steel tower, an energy kite eliminates 90 percent of the materials used in a conventional wind turbine, resulting in lower costs."[37]

The Makani energy kite has the appearance of a small plane. The kite consists of a large wing with attached rotors that would work like helicopter propellers, launching the kite into the air. The kite would be able to operate at altitudes of 330 to 1,310 feet (100 to 400 m). A computer system equipped with sensors, including a Global Positioning System (GPS) device, would help guide the kite. A tether would connect the kite to a ground station. Wind would spin the kite's wing, which would cause the kite to move in circles like the blades on a conventional turbine. Wind would also rotate the small rotors on the kite wing, and this rotation would activate a generator, converting the rotational energy into electricity.

Another type of airborne turbine that could be deployed offshore is a tethered drone. Swiss start-up company TwingTec is developing a product it calls a "twing," short for "tethered wing."[38] The twing has the appearance of a small airplane, with a wing that spans 50 feet

(15 m). Small propellers in the wing of the drone would lift it into the air up to approximately 985 feet (300 m). The drone would be connected to a platform on the ground by a tether. The drone would fly in a figure-eight pattern, pulling on the tether. Inside the platform, the tether would spin around a wheel and axle. The platform would be connected to a generator, and the generator would convert the rotational energy into electricity.

Airborne Alternatives—Inflatable Systems

Other technology companies are developing innovative airborne turbine designs modeled to look and operate like balloons or **dirigibles**. The leader within this market is Altaeros Energies, a company founded by researchers at the Massachusetts Institute of Technology. Altaeros Energies' model is called a Buoyant Airborne Turbine (BAT). The Altaeros BAT consists of a giant, 50- by 50-foot (15- by 15-m) helium-filled inflatable shell made from durable, high-strength fabric. Inside the shell is a lightweight, horizontal-axis turbine with three blades. Wind turns the blades, and aerodynamic forces lift the shell up higher in the atmosphere. The shell can reach heights of 1,000 to 2,000 feet (305 to 610 m). High-strength tethers connect the shell to the ground and keep it steady. An automated control system detects wind speeds and adjusts the shell's altitude to harness the strongest available winds. The rotor in the BAT's lightweight turbine operates like a conventional horizontal-axis turbine;

> **WORDS IN CONTEXT**
>
> **dirigibles**
> Self-guided airships that are able to fly because they are lighter than air.

wind turns the blades, and the rotational energy spins a generator, which converts the energy to electricity.

Altaeros is currently testing its BAT system in a remote region of Alaska. While a conventional wind turbine would be subject to maintenance issues in such cold conditions, Altaeros believes that its BAT system would be able to withstand these conditions and continue to operate at the same efficiency. A member of the company describes the company's goals for its BAT system:

> What we're trying to do is build something that expands wind energy to new places where it's never worked before. There have been island countries we've talked to that are worried that if their oil tanker doesn't show up, then they lose power. So folks are trying to take more control of their own energy and their own resources so there is less dependency on things outside their control.[39]

Inspired by Nature

As engineers and energy companies seek to develop new technologies that will address the disadvantages of conventional wind turbines, some are experimenting with designs that mimic nature. A team of researchers from various universities and from Sandia National Laboratories, an engineering and science laboratory managed by an agency within the Department of Energy, is currently designing efficient turbine blades that could work with 50-megawatt offshore wind turbines. A 50-megawatt turbine would generate more than six times the power of the largest turbines currently in operation.

"The US has great offshore wind energy potential, but offshore installations are expensive, so larger turbines are needed to capture that energy at an affordable cost," explained blade designer Todd Griffith.[40] In order to generate this much power, the turbine's blades would each need to be more than 650 feet (200 m) long, or longer than the length of two football fields. This is two and a half times longer than any existing turbine blade. Longer blades, however, have a greater risk of stress and damage from strong winds.

High-Rise Wind Turbines

Since wind power is greater at higher altitudes, some engineers and developers have experimented with wind turbine models that can be mounted on tall, high-rise buildings. The purpose of these high-rise turbines is to generate electricity to meet some of the building's power needs. In 2008, the Bahrain World Trade Center became the first high-rise building to incorporate commercial wind turbines into its design. The Bahrain World Trade Center is a 787-foot (240-m) skyscraper located in the city of Manama, Bahrain. Three large-scale turbines were built along bridges that connect the skyscraper's two towers. The turbines each have the capability to generate 225 kilowatts of electricity, or enough to supply between 10 and 15 percent of the building's electrical needs. The turbines are currently matching these expectations. However, other high-rise turbine projects have not been as successful. In 2010, three turbines were installed atop the 485-foot (148-m) Strata Tower, a skyscraper in London. Each turbine has five blades, and the building's developers predicted that the turbines would altogether generate 8 percent of the building's electrical needs. However, the turbine blades atop the Strata rarely turn. Furthermore, when they do turn, some residents in the building's apartment complexes have complained about the noise generated by the vibrations of the blades.

Some modern skyscrapers incorporate wind turbines into their design. Scientists and engineers are still studying how practical these might be.

To address this problem, researchers drew inspiration from palm trees. The trunk of a palm tree is made up of cylindrical segments that allow it to bend without breaking in fierce winds, including hurricane-force winds. Similar to the trunk of a palm tree, the long blades would be segmented, which would distribute loads more equally along the blade as well as enable the blade to be more flexible. In addition, a hinge near the turbine's hub would respond to changes in wind speed. If wind approaches speeds that could damage the turbine's blades, the blades could fold and align themselves in the direction of the wind. When a turbine's blades are against the wind, they are more vulnerable to damage than when the blades are aligned with the wind. For this reason, maintenance costs for this turbine model would likely be less than maintenance costs for a conventional turbine. These segmented turbine blades are also designed to spread out more when wind speeds are low, which maximizes energy production. Because these segmented blades could withstand extreme winds, they could be used along the coasts of areas that are often hard-hit by severe storms such as hurricanes.

Bladeless Turbines

An innovative technology company in Spain is exploring bladeless turbines. Start-up company Vortex Bladeless is developing a number of these prototypes. The Vortex turbine model consists of a long, cylindrical tube made of fiberglass and carbon fiber. The tube would be mounted vertically, like a conventional turbine tower. Wind would blow around the tube, and the wind behind the structure would form a whirlpool, or vortex. The vortex would exert force on the tube, which would cause it to oscillate, or move back and forth. This movement would travel to a carbon fiber rod at the bottom of the structure. The rod would move inside a linear alternator, which would convert the kinetic energy into electricity.

One benefit of a bladeless turbine such as Vortex Bladeless's model is that it would likely pose less risk to birds than a conventional turbine since spinning blades are the cause of avian fatalities. Also, since bladeless turbines would require less material and fewer components than conventional turbines, bladeless models would cost less to manufacture, transport, and maintain. However, a disadvantage of not having blades is that bladeless turbines would not be able to sweep as large an area as conventional turbines. Thus, bladeless turbines could not capture as much wind energy as conventional turbines. Additionally, while Vortex Bladeless claims that their turbines will operate silently, some critics are skeptical of this. If bladeless turbines do produce a significant amount of noise, consumers may be reluctant to live in areas near them. Sheila Widnall, an aeronautics and astronautics professor at the Massachusetts Institute of Technology, explains:

Bladeless turbines look dramatically different from typical wind turbines. A prototype was installed in Spain in 2015.

> [W]hen the cylinder gets very big and wind gets very high, you get a range of frequencies. You won't be able to get as much energy out of it as you want to because the oscillation is fundamentally turbulent. The oscillating frequencies that shake the cylinder will make noise. It will sound like a freight train coming through your wind farm.[41]

But other experts, such as Stanford University engineering professor John Dabiri, see the promise in Vortex's bladeless turbines. Dabiri remarks: "Anyone who says the three-bladed turbine is the best we can do is lacking in vision."[42]

A World Powered by Wind

Since the early years of commercial wind power, innovative thinkers have made major advances in the field. In the late 1800s, inventors developed the first windmills to convert wind energy into electricity. Within the last few decades, scientists have developed advanced technologies for both offshore and onshore wind. Modern wind power systems can harness powerful winds from farther out at sea and at greater heights in the air. Some portable systems promise to bring more power to remote communities and to the developing world.

Wind power offers great advantages over fossil fuels. As fossil fuels become depleted within the next century and as governments around the world explore ways to combat climate change, wind power has become an increasingly attractive option. Wind is a free, easily accessible source of energy that does not emit greenhouse gases. As technology advances and prices drop, more countries are developing their wind power industries. By the end of 2016, the countries with the most installed wind capacity were China, the United States, Germany, and India. Global installed wind capacity grew by 12.6 percent from 2015 to 2016, and the GWEC predicted that future growth will continue to be strong. At the end of the year 2016, GWEC secretary general Steve Sawyer concluded:

Wind power is now successfully competing with heavily subsidized incumbents across the globe, building new industries, creating hundreds of thousands of jobs and leading the way towards a clean energy future. We are well into a period of disruptive change, moving away from power systems centered on a few large, polluting plants towards markets increasingly dominated by a range of widely distributed renewable energy sources.[43]

The growth of the global wind power industry will be determined by a number of factors. These include technological improvements, economic gain, and government policies. Considering industry predictions and the current rate of growth, wind power appears to have a strong and promising future.

INTRODUCTION: BLOCK ISLAND WIND FARM

1. "Block Island Wind Farm," *Deepwater Wind*, 2017. www.dwwind.com.

2. Quoted in Christopher Helman, "Is America's First Offshore Wind Farm a Real Revolution or Just Another Green Boondoggle?" *Forbes*, April 20, 2016. www.forbes.com.

3. Quoted in Tatiana Schlossberg, "America's First Offshore Wind Farm Spins to Life," *New York Times*, December 14, 2016. www.nytimes.com.

4. Quoted in Quentin Hardy, "Google Says It Will Run Entirely on Renewable Energy in 2017," *New York Times*, December 6, 2016. www.nytimes.com.

5. Quoted in Jess Shankleman, Brian Parkin, and Anna Hirtenstein, "Gigantic Wind Turbines Signal Era of Subsidy-Free Green Power," *Bloomberg*, April 21, 2017. www.bloomberg.com.

CHAPTER 1: HOW DOES WIND POWER WORK?

6. "History of U.S. Wind Energy," *US Department of Energy*, n.d. www.energy.gov.

7. "History of Wind Energy," *Wind Energy Foundation*, n.d. www.windenergyfoundation.org.

8. Quoted in "Why Do Wind Turbines Have Three Narrow Blades, but Ceiling Fans Have Five Wide Blades?" *Scientific American*, February 2009. www.scientificamerican.com.

9. Quoted in "Improved Savonius Wind Turbine Captures Wind in the Cities," *Science Daily*, May 20, 2016. www.sciencedaily.com.

10. Quoted in Jane Silcock, "Wind Farms Generate Power, Revenue, Say MU Extension Specialists," *University of Missouri Extension*, July 14, 2008. www.missouri.edu.

11. Quoted in Tom Dart and Oliver Milman, "'The Wild West of Wind': Republicans Push Texas as Unlikely Green Energy Leader," *Guardian*, February 20, 2017. www.theguardian.com.

12. "Global Statistics," *Global Wind Energy Council*, 2016. www.gwec.net.

13. Quoted in Javier C. Hernández, "It Can Power a Small Nation. But This Wind Farm in China Is Mostly Idle," *New York Times*, January 15, 2017. www.nytimes.com.

14. Quoted in Anmar Frangoul, "China Continues to Lead Global Wind Energy Market, Says New Report," *CNBC*, April 26, 2017. www.cnbc.com.

CHAPTER 2: CAN WIND POWER REPLACE FOSSIL FUELS?

15. "US Energy Facts Explained," *US Energy Information Administration*, May 19, 2017. www.eia.gov.

16. "A Brief History of Coal Use," *US Department of Energy*, February 12, 2013. www.fossil.energy.gov.

17. "How Much Gasoline Does the United States Consume?" *US Energy Information Administration*, March 29, 2017. www.eia.gov.

18. "What's the Difference Between Weather and Climate?" *NASA*, February 1, 2005. www.nasa.gov.

19. Quoted in "Interview: The Way Forward after Deepwater Horizon Spill," *World Maritime News*, January 28, 2015. www.worldmaritimenews.com.

20. Quoted in Chris Tomlinson, "Houston Startup Plans to Store Wind Energy Underground," *Houston Chronicle*, July 7, 2017. www.houstonchronicle.com.

21. Quoted in Ashley Halsey III, "Aging Power Grid on Overload as US Demands More Electricity," *Washington Post*, August 1, 2012. www.washingtonpost.com.

22. Quoted in Emma Bryce, "Will Wind Turbines Ever Be Safe for Birds?" *Audubon*, March 16, 2016. www.audubon.org.

23. Quoted in Devin Henry, "Grassley: Trump Will Attack Wind Energy 'Over My Dead Body,'" *The Hill*, August 31, 2016. www.thehill.com.

24. "Renewables Can Replace Fossil Fuels by 2050," *Sun & Wind Energy*, September 22, 2015. www.sunwindenergy.com.

CHAPTER 3: HOW DOES OFFSHORE COMPARE WITH ONSHORE WIND?

25. Quoted in Adam Vaughan, "Mersey Feat: World's Biggest Wind Turbines Go Online Near Liverpool," *Guardian*, May 17, 2017. www.theguardian.com.

26. "World's Most Powerful Wind Turbine Once Again Smashes 24 Hour Power Generation Record," *MHI Vestas Offshore Wind*, January 27, 2017. www.mhivestasoffshore.com.

27. Quoted in "Onshore Wind Energy: What Are the Pros and Cons?" *Guardian*, September 25, 2012. www.theguardian.com.

28. Quoted in Gino Fanelli, "OC Offshore Meteorological Tower Step Toward Wind Farm," *USA Today*, March 1, 2017. www.usatoday.com.

29. Quoted in Trent Knoss, "Offshore Wind Turbines Vulnerable to Category 5 Hurricane Gusts," *CU Boulder Today*, June 7, 2017. www.colorado.edu.

30. Quoted in "Impact of Offshore Wind Farms on Marine Species," *Science Daily*, October 16, 2014. www.sciencedaily.com.

31. Quoted in "Impact of Offshore Wind Farms on Marine Species."

32. Quoted in Mary Ann Bragg, "Labor, Environmentalists Tout First US Offshore Wind Farm," *Cape Cod Times*, June 14, 2017. www.capecodtimes.com.

33. Quoted in Pilitia Clark, "Developing Countries Begin to Take Lead in Green Energy Growth," *Financial Times*, October 27, 2014. www.ft.com.

CHAPTER 4: WHAT IS THE FUTURE OF WIND POWER?

34. Quoted in Nathalie Thomas, "World's First Floating Wind Farm Towed to North Sea Base," *Financial Times*, August 2, 2017. www.ft.com.

35. "Statoil to Build the World's First Floating Wind Farm: Hywind Scotland," *Statoil*, n.d. www.statoil.com.

36. Quoted in Adam Vaughan, "World's First Floating Windfarm to Take Shape off Coast of Scotland," *Guardian*, June 27, 2017. www.theguardian.com.

37. "Learn More about Makani's Energy Kite," *Makani*, n.d. www.x.company/makani.

38. Quoted in Ellsworth Dickson, "TwingTec Designs Innovative Remote Power System," *ResourceWorld*, 2016. www.twingtec.ch.

39. Quoted in Thom Patterson, "Meet the BAT, an Airborne Wind Turbine," *CNN*, May 12, 2014. www.cnn.com.

40. Quoted in "Enormous Blades Could Lead to More Offshore Energy in US," *Sandia Labs*, January 28, 2016. www.sandia.gov.

41. Quoted in Phil McKenna, "Bladeless Wind Turbines May Offer More Form than Function," *MIT Technology Review*, May 27, 2015. www.technologyreview.com.

42. Quoted in McKenna, "Bladeless Wind Turbines May Offer More Form than Function."

43. Quoted in "Global Wind Report 2016," *Global Wind Energy Council*, 2016. www.gwec.net.

BOOKS

John Allen, *Careers in Environmental and Energy Technology.* San Diego, CA: ReferencePoint, 2017.

Lester R. Brown, *The Great Transition: Shifting from Fossil Fuels to Solar and Wind Energy.* New York: W.W. Norton & Company, 2015.

Matt Doeden, *Green Energy: Crucial Gains or Economic Strains?* Minneapolis, MN: Twenty-First Century Books, 2010.

Melissa Higgins, *Wind Energy.* Minneapolis, MN: Abdo Publishing, 2013.

Stuart A. Kallen, *Cutting Edge Energy Technology.* San Diego, CA: ReferencePoint, 2017.

Andrea C. Nakaya, *What Is the Future of Wind Power?* San Diego, CA: ReferencePoint, 2013.

WEBSITES

Bureau of Labor Statistics: Careers in Wind Energy
https://www.bls.gov/green/wind_energy

The website of the Bureau of Labor Statistics, the US government agency that studies the nation's workforce, provides information about promising careers in the growing wind energy job market.

Department of Energy: Renewable Energy
https://energy.gov/science-innovation/energy-sources/renewable-energy

The website of the Department of Energy, the US agency that promotes innovative energy policies, features information about all kinds of renewable energy sources, including wind power.

Global Wind Energy Council
http://www.gwec.net

The Global Wind Energy Council's comprehensive website includes news about the latest wind energy projects, statistics about the global wind power market, and annual reports on the status of the wind power industry.

New York Times: Wind Power
https://www.nytimes.com/topic/subject/wind-power

This news feed gives updates on the latest stories about wind power from the *New York Times.* Learn about the companies, scientists, engineers, and politicians who are shaping the future of wind power.

Windpower Monthly Magazine
http://www.windpowermonthly.com

The website of *Windpower Monthly* magazine features the latest stories on wind energy projects and technologies.

ABOUT THE AUTHOR

Maddie Spalding has written more than 20 books for children. She graduated from Augustana University in 2013 with degrees in English and Psychology. Spalding also studied children's literature at the University of Roehampton in London, England. She lives in Minnesota with her husband.